Item
sho

Colds, Flu
and Other Infections

Angela Royston

W

FRANKLIN WATTS

LONDON • SYDNEY

This edition 2010

First published in 2006 by
Franklin Watts
338 Euston Road
London NW1 3BH

Franklin Watts Australia
Level 17/207 Kent Street
Sydney NSW 2000

Produced by Calcium, New Brook House, 385 Alfreton Road, Nottingham, NG7 5LR

Editor: Sarah Eason
Design: Paul Myerscough
Illustration: Annie Boberg and Geoff Ward
Picture research: Sarah Jameson
Consultant: Dr Stephen Earwicker

Acknowledgements:
The publisher would like to thank the following for permission to reproduce photographs:
Alamy p.10, p.16, p.19, p.20, ; Istockphoto p.7; CMSP p.11, p.25; Inmagine p.13, p.26;
Tudor Photography p.8, p.15, p.22, p.23, p.27; Chris Fairclough Photography p.6, p.9, p.12,
p.14, p.17, p.18, p.21, p.24.

Every attempt has been made to clear copyright. Should there be any inadvertent omission
please apply to the publisher for rectification.

A CIP catalogue record for this book is available from the British Library.

Dewey Decimal Classification Number: 616.2

ISBN: 978 1 4451 0165 1

Printed in China

Franklin Watts is a division of
Hachette Children's Books,
an Hachette UK company.
www.hachette.co.uk

Contents

What are colds and flu?

Colds and flu are illnesses that affect your throat, nose and chest.

When someone has a cold they usually sneeze and have a sore throat, a runny nose and a cough. A cold lasts between one and two weeks.

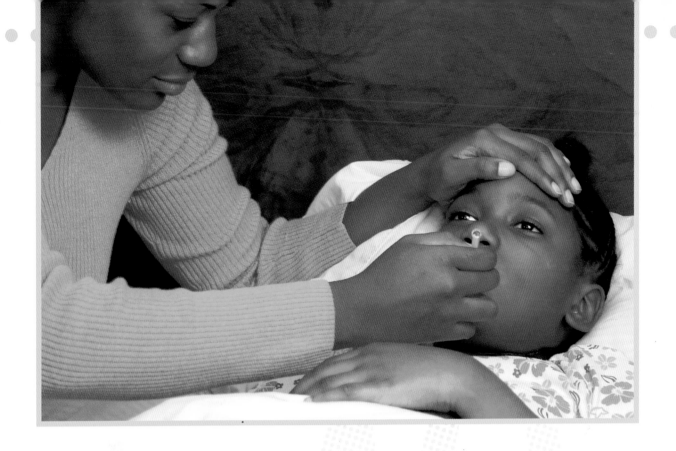

Flu is worse than a cold because your muscles ache and you feel tired. You also have a **fever**. This means that your body becomes much hotter than usual, yet you may shiver and feel cold at the same time.

Why do you shiver when you have a fever?

The air around you feels cold when you have a fever, because your body is hot. Shivering is its way of trying to warm up, even though it needs to cool down!

Why do colds and flu affect your breathing?

When someone has a cold or flu, thick liquid called **mucus** may block their nose. The mucus makes it difficult to **breathe**.

When you have a cold or flu, your nose and some of the **airways** in your **lungs** become filled with mucus. Your nose may be so full of thick mucus – or snot – that you cannot breathe through it.

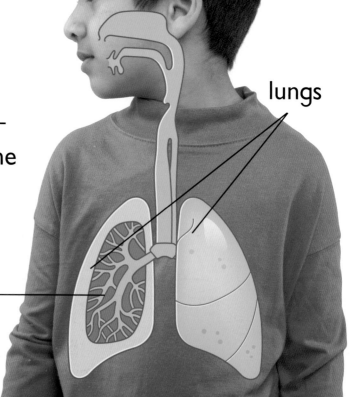

lungs

airway

Colds and flu can also make people cough. Coughing is the body's way of getting rid of anything that might be blocking the airways.

Tickly coughs are caused by swelling in your throat. The swelling makes your body think that your throat is blocked, which is why you cough. Chesty coughs are caused by mucus in your lungs. When you cough, the mucus is loosened.

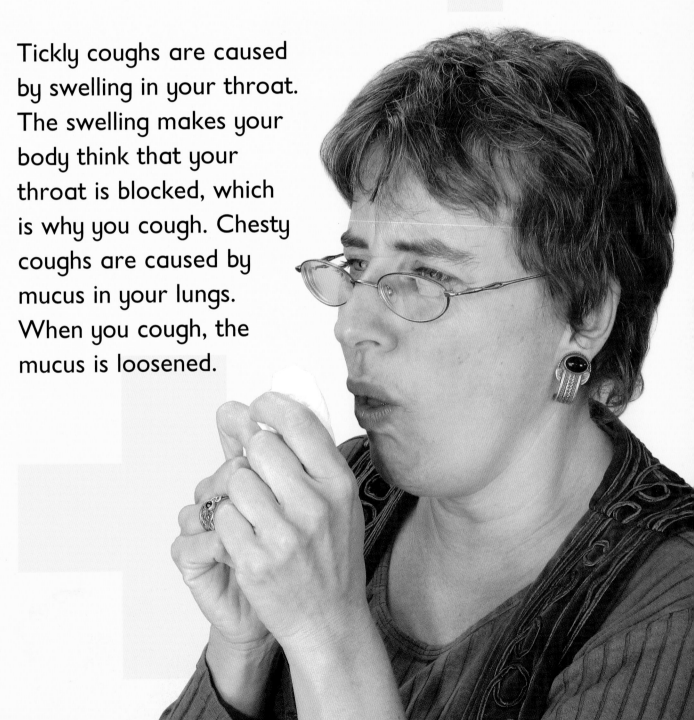

What causes colds and flu?

Very tiny **germs** called **viruses** cause colds and flu.

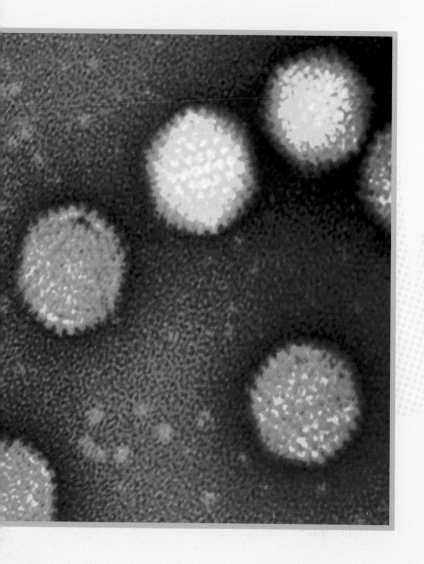

A virus is so small it can only be seen under a microscope. A microscope is a machine that makes things look much bigger than they actually are. This is what a cold virus looks like under a powerful microscope.

Tiny viruses

Viruses are the smallest living things – it would take two million of them to cover the head of a pin! They float easily through the air because they are so light.

Your airways are lined with tiny hairs and mucus. The hairs push the mucus through the airway. This is what the tiny hairs look like under a microscope. Your body makes extra mucus when you have a cold or flu to wash away the germs inside your airways.

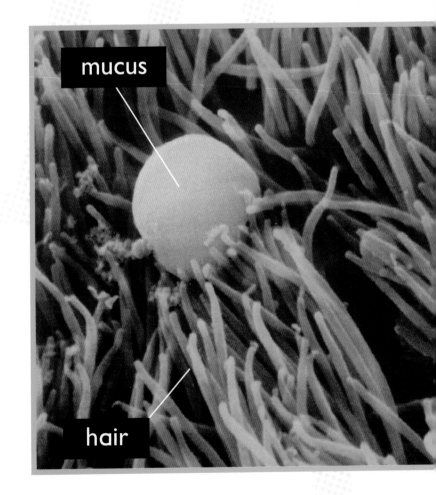

mucus

hair

How are colds and flu treated?

Resting and drinking lots of water will help to treat a cold or flu.

When you have a cold, you should keep warm and drink plenty of water. You need to drink to replace the water your body loses through making mucus. Putting a few drops of salty water in your nostrils can help to unblock your nose.

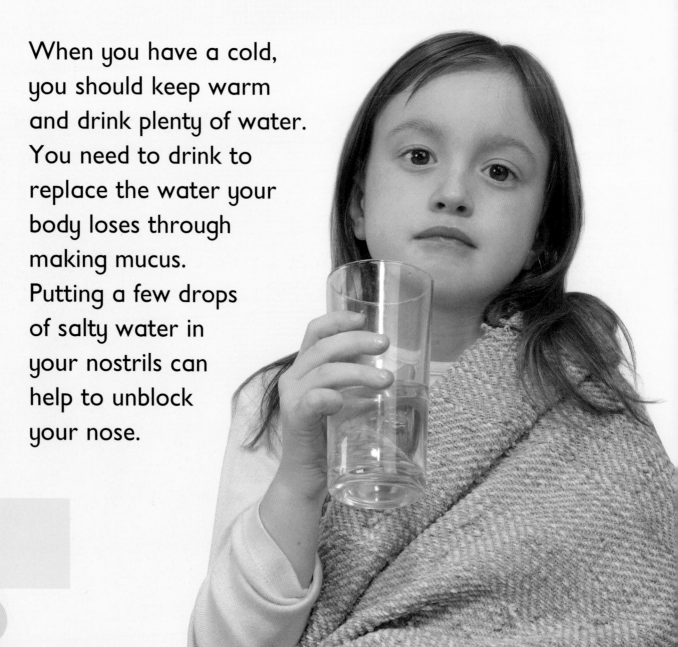

Flu can make you feel very ill. If you catch flu it is best to stay in bed. Sleeping will give your body a chance to deal with the illness.

How you can help:

+ Remember to drink lots of water.
+ Rest.
+ Stay in bed if you have flu.

Which medicines help to treat colds and flu?

Painkillers and cough medicines may make people feel better, but they don't cure a cold or flu.

A painkiller stops your head aching and makes your throat feel less sore. It can also help to bring down a high **temperature**.

Take care!

Only ever take a medicine given to you by your parent or carer. It is important to follow the instructions carefully. People should never take more medicine than shown in the instructions, or another dose too soon after the last one.

Cough medicine helps to stop coughing. Medicine for a tickly cough soothes the throat. Medicine for a chesty cough helps to clear the mucus in the lungs.

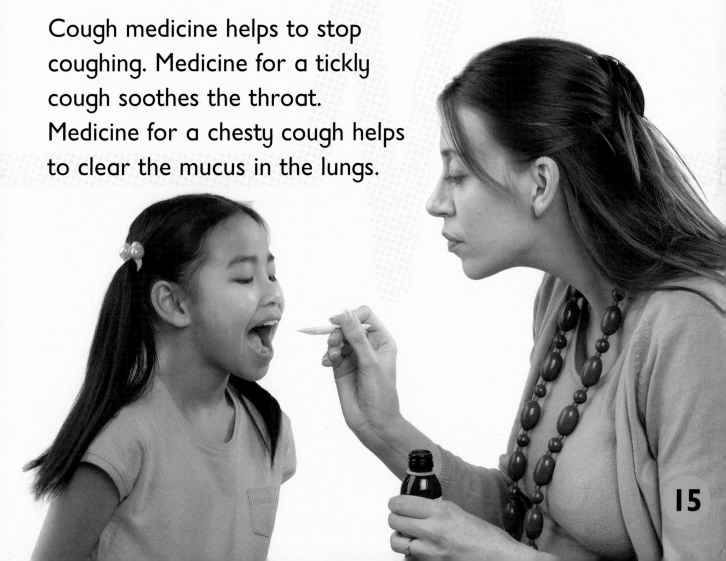

How are colds and flu caught?

The most usual way to catch a cold or flu is by breathing in the viruses through your nose or mouth.

When someone with a cold sneezes, germs spray into the air. They float in the air and can easily be breathed in by someone else. Some viruses land on things around you. They cling to your fingers if you touch them.

When someone with a cold coughs, germs spray into the air and you may breathe them in. If some germs get on your fingers and you touch your face, the germs can then get into your nose or mouth.

Try this!

Squirt water out of a water pistol or an old washing-up liquid bottle. How far does the water go? When you sneeze or cough, millions of germs shoot out of your nose or mouth with just as much force!

17

Can you stop colds and flu spreading?

You can stop germs spreading by covering your mouth and nose when you sneeze and cough. Washing your hands helps too.

Throw used tissues into a bin. If you leave them lying around, the germs on them can float into the air and give someone else your cold or flu.

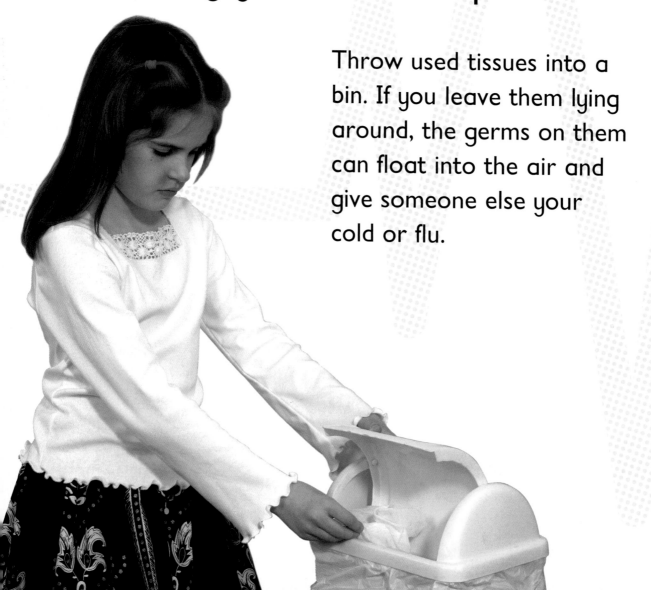

When you sneeze, cough or blow your nose, lots of germs get on to your hands. Wash your hands as often as possible so that you do not spread germs when you touch things.

How you can help:

+ Remember to cover your nose or mouth when you sneeze or cough.
+ Put used tissues into a bin with a lid.
+ Wash your hands regularly.

Do colds and flu cause other illnesses?

Sometimes you may get a chest **infection** or ear infection after you have had a cold or flu.

Ear infections and chest infections are often caused by germs called **bacteria**. This is what the bacteria that cause chest infections look like under a microscope.

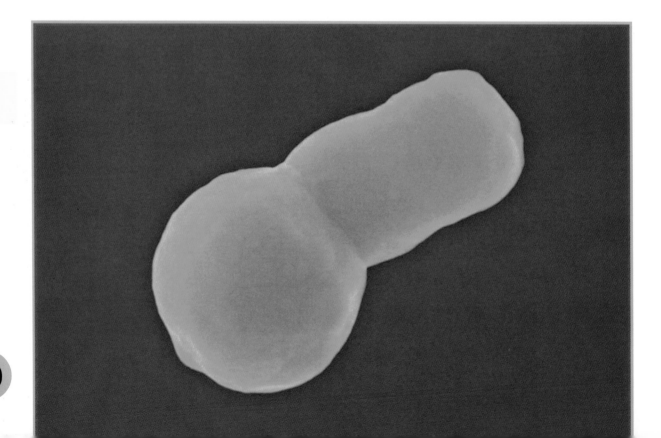

Bacteria

Bacteria are very small, but not as small as viruses. Each one can split in half to make two bacteria. Each of those bacteria then split to make more bacteria. This is how a few bacteria can quickly become thousands of bacteria.

An ear infection can give you very bad earache. It is caused by bacteria in your ear. A chest infection can lead to a bad cough and your chest may ache. This is caused by bacteria in your lungs.

21

How do doctors treat other infections?

A doctor may give you a medicine called an **antibiotic** to kill the bacteria that cause infection.

Antibiotics are special medicines that you usually take by swallowing them. Antibiotics kill the bacteria that cause infections, but they cannot kill viruses.

When your parent or carer gives you an antibiotic, it is very important that you follow the instructions. You may feel better after a few days but you must keep taking the antibiotic for as long as your doctor tells you to.

Take care!

Antibiotics should only be taken if a doctor tells you to. It is important to follow the doctor's instructions. If too little medicine is taken, it will not kill all the bacteria. If the antibiotics are stopped too soon, some of the bacteria will go on living and can make people ill again.

What are stomach upsets?

When you have a stomach upset you may be sick or have **diarrhoea**.

Stomach upsets are caused by germs in your stomach. Germs get into your stomach through your mouth. Germs can live on food or on something you put in your mouth. They can also float in the air. People sometimes get a stomach upset when they have a cold or flu.

You should always wash your hands after using the toilet and before eating food. Washing your hands washes away the germs that can cause stomach upsets.

How you can help:

+ Drink plenty of water. The water will replace liquid lost by being sick or having diarrhoea.
+ Eat only plain food, such as salted crackers and plain rice. Plain food is easier for your stomach to deal with.

How can you prevent colds and flu?

You are less likely to catch a cold or flu if you keep your body healthy.

Eat healthy food, such as lots of fruit and vegetables. Healthy food helps your body to work well, which means it can deal with colds, flu and other infections.

How you can help:

+ Eat plenty of fruit and vegetables.
+ Drink eight cups of water or other liquid every day.
+ Take plenty of exercise that makes you puff.
+ Wash your hands after using the toilet and before eating or drinking.
+ Sleep well.

You are more likely to get ill when you are very tired. Sleep allows your body time to recover and this helps you to stay well. People sleep best when they go to bed at about the same time each night. Adults need to sleep for about eight hours. Children need to sleep for longer.

Glossary

airway   tube in the lungs through which air passes.

antibiotic   medicine that kills bacteria.

bacteria   tiny living things, some of which can make you ill.

breathe   to take in and let out air through the mouth and nose.

diarrhoea   when the solid waste your body makes (your poo) is loose and runny.

fever   when an infection makes your body temperature higher than usual.

germ   tiny living thing that can make you ill.

infection   illness caused by germs.

lung   part of the body that breathes in and breathes out air.

mucus   thick liquid made by the body. Mucus comes out of your nose when it is runny.

painkiller   medicine that stops you feeling pain.

temperature   how hot or cold something is. When you have a temperature your body is much hotter than usual.

virus   germ. Some viruses cause colds and flu.

Find out more

A fun children's website about colds:
www.kidshealth.org/kid/ill_injure/sick/colds.html

Find out all about flu:
www.kidshealth.org/kid/ill_injure/flu/flu.html

An American website about flu:
www.noah-health.org/en/lung/
conditions/influenza

Index